T0063149

Manifest
ANYTHING
YOU WANT IN
30
—— Days —

VICKIE EMANUELE

BALBOA

PRESS

A DIVISION OF HAY HOUSE

Balboa Press books may be ordered through booksellers or by contacting:

Balboa Press
A Division of Hay House
1663 Liberty Drive
Bloomington, IN 47403
www.balboapress.com
1-(877) 407-4847

Because of the dynamic nature of the Internet, any web addresses or
links contained in this book may have changed since publication and
may no longer be valid. The views expressed in this work are solely those
of the author and do not necessarily reflect the views of the publisher,
and the publisher hereby disclaims any responsibility for them.

The author of this book does not dispense medical advice or prescribe the use
of any technique as a form of treatment for physical, emotional, or medical
problems without the advice of a physician, either directly or indirectly. The
intent of the author is only to offer information of a general nature to help
you in your quest for emotional and spiritual well-being. In the event you use
any of the information in this book for yourself, which is your constitutional
right, the author and the publisher assume no responsibility for your actions.

Any people depicted in stock imagery provided by Thinkstock are models,
and such images are being used for illustrative purposes only.
Certain stock imagery © Thinkstock.

Printed in the United States of America.

ISBN: 978-1-4525-6576-7 (sc)
ISBN: 978-1-4525-6575-0 (e)

Balboa Press rev. date: 3/20/2013

WARNING: READING THIS BOOK AND PERFORMING THE FOLLOWING PRACTICES MAY RESULT IN **LIVING YOUR DREAM LIFE!**

I will teach you how to:

THINK IT

FEEL IT

SEE IT

HAVE IT

BECOME IT

These are the steps to manifesting. Just turn the page to learn how to make your dreams come true.

Table of Contents

FOREWORD

You are about to embark on a journey that took me many, many years to realize. I hope that you can reduce this time and learn the powers of manifestation and bring joy and happiness to your life. I assure you that if you follow the techniques and utilize the tools presented here then all of your dreams will come true.

I had the author at my disposal every day and every night for years. I was told to do this and do that. Watch your words and think positively. I resisted and did not take these requests to heart. Of course, when your wife is telling you these things it is different than when you hear it from an independent source. Finally, I gave up resistance and followed her advice, which she has summarized in *Manifest ANYTHING You Want in 30 Days*.

I am an optometrist, which means I attended school for 8 years after high school. It is a long time to devote to your education only to find out that after about 7 years of practicing that maybe there is something I would rather be doing. I resisted and continued to struggle with the same routine day in and day out. How could I change careers? I still have school loans and what would others think of me? My wife always supported me in trying something new and attracting a new opportunity to me. I did not listen. I continued to practice unhappily another 8 years.

Finally, I got to a point where my health, my family, my finances, my career and my emotional well-being were being affected by this lack of passion with my career. I began to follow Vickie's advice and everything has changed. And changed quickly.

I have a tremendous amount of energy. I enjoy my family every day and have a wonderful, close relationship with my wife. My credit card debt has virtually disappeared while not making any more money. I sold my practice and received a job offer on the same day. I have never felt better in my life.

I want to address my resistance to my career a little more specifically to demonstrate the power of manifestation and how you too can have anything that you want. As I mentioned, I was an optometrist for almost 15 years. I was doing well financially but had no passion and going into work felt like a chore. Anyone else feel this way? I finally decided to give myself a chance for change and started with some affirmations (you will learn about these later.) I watched what I said and felt how leaving my current position would feel. And it felt good. I was in a practice in a commercial setting so I was unsure how I could sell it, what the value was and anybody I spoke with never heard of selling such a practice. I ignored all the negatives and focused on the positives. I placed my practice for sale and sold it for the asking price within two weeks.

Now what? I didn't sell it for enough to retire so I needed a new job. I searched and made some contacts for a new position that I thought would be great. I applied for the position and went through the interview process. I knew there were other candidates so I stayed positive and saw myself in that new position. As I was leaving the bank after receiving the funds on the practice sale, I received a call from my boss informing me that I got the job. AWESOME!!! So this is how all this manifestation stuff works. I wish I had listened sooner but better late than never.

I am stubborn and not inclined to change. Well, I guess I should say I use to be stubborn and not inclined to change. In the last 3 months, I have sold my practice of 13 years, received a job as a sales representative never having been in sales before and I am moving across the country. I have never been happier and had more passion and interest in life and what it has to offer. I ask you to be open and follow the path presented by Vickie to get anything you want. Good luck.

Ken Emanuele, O.D.

INTRODUCTION: WHAT IS MANIFESTING?

You've heard it before. You could get what you want in life . . . if you just knew how to manifest it.

So what is manifesting? Well, it's really very simple.

Manifesting is the act of wanting something and then bringing it into reality. In other words, you don't just dream it. You achieve it.

One word of warning: what you will manifest in the next 30 days with the help of this book must be attainable and reachable. I'd also like to point out that you should start with just one thing that you want, and make it happen, instead of trying to manifest ten things at the same time. You need to focus, because manifesting isn't something that's done in leaps and bounds. It's all in the baby steps.

I promise you that what you want is within your grasp. In other words, you can reach your own mountain peak.

Let's say you want to be a multimillionaire, but you've spent years trying to pay both the mortgage and the electric bill. Deep down, you don't really think great wealth is truly attainable. You might want it, but your mind is screaming, "You will never reach this goal!"

Now, I'd like to challenge those negative feelings. As you progress through the next 30 days, I won't ask you to manifest $1 million, but instead, think about bringing in an extra $400 a month . . . and then $1,000 . . . and then $10,000.

Remember: it's all about the baby steps.

I know that you'll get to the top, but remember, life isn't about crossing that goal line. It's about playing the game and placing one foot in front of the other.

It's time to move your thinking upward, from your feet to your mind.

One of the most important lessons I will teach you over the next 30 days is that if you think something is impossible, then it will be. Whatever you believe to be true is your reality. If you believe it, then it will happen.

***

Before we get started, I'd also like to give you some very good news: You're not exactly new to manifesting. In fact, people manifest all the time, but they just don't realize it. You manifested owning your home and starting that small business, if that applies to you. You even made sure you got married and had those gorgeous kids.

What you focused on was then brought (by you) into reality. And it was probably as easy as manifesting a new pair of Jimmy Choos or a move across the country for your family.

Who made it possible?

Just one person: you!

WHY SHOULD YOU MANIFEST?

The purpose of this book is to help you become aware of how you're already manifesting, help you sharpen your skills, and then guide you into bringing abundance into all areas of your life.

Manifesting abundance in your life is your birthright. It's also a way of living that will become secondhand the longer you do it and the more you expand your mind.

This book will help you expand your way of thinking, let go of limiting belief systems, and bring in self-worth and self-love. Within these pages, I will prove to you that your dreams aren't just lofty ideas, but will become life priorities. In this daily guide broken down over 30 days, I'll teach you how manifesting really works and make it easy for you to do it again and again.

The idea behind this book is that you can do this 30-day plan over and over again to continue adding to your life's blessings. It won't take long until you have created everything you've ever wanted in your life.

WHY YOU ARE THE ANSWER

Perhaps you've noticed a strange phenomenon that dictates what happens in your world. Think about what you've focused on in life—both positive and negative. Think about how those two different types of emotions have snowballed into either thrillingly positive or extremely negative responses.

I'm sure you've heard the saying "You will get what you focus on." This book will make sure you know that those words are true.

So true.

Let's take the case of Emily, a 42-year-old wife, mother, and teacher from Ohio. She tells anyone who will listen that her life is devoid of joy, hope, and prosperity. Guess what? She lives the very existence that she describes because she's making that life come true.

Maybe you tell yourself that life is without joy, excitement, or challenges. Or you convince yourself that the old song Is That All There Is? Should be your theme song.

Some of us tell ourselves on a daily basis how fat and unattractive we are . . . and then we walk around looking the way we feel and fit the mold we're describing.

Perhaps you tell others that you really want to be in a loving relationship, but say that there's "no one out there" for you. The years slip by and you still haven't found a companion. Why? Because you made that situation come true, too.

Remember this rule of the Universe: whatever energy you focus on will be the exact scenario you actually create.

If you say it and think it . . . you will live it.

I'm making you aware of these facts because if you want to manifest something different in your life, you need to tell yourself and others what your new story is all about and how you're going to make it happen. If you declare a new story for your life, so it is.

And you can rewrite your story today.

For example, if you start telling yourself how wonderful and abundant you are and how joyful and beautiful your life has become, then you will own that life.

So what will you tell yourself today?

YOU ARE WHAT YOU MANIFEST

What's amazing is that you're already a master at manifesting. In fact, you've already manifested several things in your life. Think of that time when you either wanted a new job doing something specific or wanted that cool pair of shoes.

The reason these things came easily to you was because you followed a process where you first had a deep belief that you could have the job or the shoes. Your thoughts and emotions were specific, clear, and headed in one direction like a speeding freight train. You were going to get what you wanted, no matter what. At night, you allowed your dreams to show you a sneak preview of the life you desired. And during the day, your thoughts were focused on the new life you wanted to live.

Then it became a reality.

You had it in your hands.

HOW MANIFESTING WORKS: A BASIC LESSON

I'd like to explain to you how manifesting really works.

Imagine that you're a television set. Your mind, thoughts, beliefs, words, and emotions are your antennae. The Universe and Spirit are the receivers and givers.

Every word, thought, emotion, and belief is constantly going out to the Universe because it knows at all times that what you're thinking, saying, and believing is true. The Universe then grants this to you as your reality. I can't stress enough how important positive thoughts and words are if you want to have a happy and satisfied life.

The Universe doesn't know good or bad. It just knows that this human being is saying, thinking, or doing things that cause it to send what you've conjured up your way.

Remember: Thoughts are very powerful energy. They are creating your life.

Bob is a salesman who has always walked around saying, "I'm so broke." So the Universe responded by saying, "Let's give Bob broke again." The point is, if you keep thinking something negative, then you're going to have a negative experience.

Everything is energy, which is just a reflection of what you say, think, and feel. Your thoughts, words, and emotions can actually transform into reality.

In today's stressful world, it takes practice and patience for some people to rid their lives of such negativity because they've been in a dark space with an attitude of lack for a long time. These people have been told a story and have then lived it, perhaps since childhood.

The good news is that if this is what you're doing, you can change it.

Despite any circumstances you currently find yourself in at this very moment, you (and only you) are responsible for your life. Therefore, you can have the abundant, healthy, loving, joyful life that you really want.

LET'S GET STARTED

I'd like you to look at the different areas of your life: money, love, health, jobs, and all relationships.

Select the best areas of your life—those that you're proud of or confident about. Now I'd like you to choose an area that needs work and bring the same positive energy to that one as you do to the good areas of your life.

Start by saying this positive affirmation: "I have an abundance of [prosperity] or [love] or [creativity]." Fill in the blank with what you want to manifest.

Next, you should think and feel with your innermost emotions: "What does this look like and feel like to me?" Remember that everyone will feel things differently. Then—and this is crucial—you must visualize, think, and feel the way you would if you already had what you're manifesting.

This is crucial. Let's say you desire prosperity. See yourself with unlimited money, going shopping, traveling, and being debt free. See that stack of cash getting bigger and bigger. I know that some of you are going to say, "Yes, that sounds nice, but I don't believe I can really have it."

In order for you to have something, you first have to believe you can have it!

I had a client who told me, "Vickie, I'm really poor."

I asked her, "Do you believe you can be abundant?"

She said, "No, not really. I'm poor because of my ex-husband. He told me I can never become abundant because I don't have the education for it."

So it is!

She just declared that her life was poor, and she didn't believe she could be abundant. So how could she expect to not be poor?

YOUR PERSONAL BELIEF SYSTEM

You learned most of your belief systems when you were a child from your parents. Some have really stuck—seemingly with Crazy Glue.

Maybe your father drilled into your head, "You have to work hard to have money."

This is a belief system. If you truly believe those words, then you will have to do exactly what you believe—work hard—to make money. In order to manifest your money in a far easier way, you'll need to tweak or even revamp your belief system, which isn't always easy.

Old belief systems are like baggage that you carry around with you every single day for years. In order to lose that baggage, you have to make a major shift.

By the way, you have belief systems that are unique to just about everything in your life—love, health, money, relationships, and so on. No belief system is bad, but if you're not getting what you want in life, then you need to take a very close look at that belief system, zeroing in on and pinpointing that area of your existence. You can change it or expand it, depending on what is limiting you.

Let's say you believe that it's going to be difficult to find the true love of your life, your soul mate. Your belief system is cemented by the idea that all your family members and friends have already told you that true love is very hard to find, and maybe you'll just have to settle for "pretty good." This is a limiting belief system.

I make sure that my clients start with baby steps because it's tough to take big leaps in this area. You are literally retraining your brain. It's not that difficult to do. Just institute a new belief system of your own, such as: "A loving relationship comes easily to me."

Keep saying this positive affirmation every single day.

Or maybe you'll want to say: "The love of my life is on his/her way to me."

The act of saying positive affirmations might feel strange or silly at first, but the more you say them, the more you'll believe them, and the more power they'll have.

Those words will become your reality.

A QUICK WORD ABOUT THE ECONOMY

I want to take a second and address the current economic condition of the world. The most popular belief system I've been hearing recently might be affecting you!

For the last few years, people have been saying that they don't believe they can have prosperity anymore because of the poor state of the world economy. This is a hugely negative belief system.

As early as 2010, clients started coming to me in droves asking when they were going to lose their jobs because of the economy. These were people that had no reason to fear a job loss. But the negativity crept in and became an actual belief system where their brains announced, "I'm going to lose my job."

The fear is everywhere, because each day we're bombarded by predominantly negative news. Our friends and family members also discuss their fears when it comes to the economy. Once you get into the fear mode, your mind takes over, and all you do is dwell on lack.

When fear enters your mind or any kind of negativity, I want you to say and think, "Cancel, cancel, cancel."

Just think of your mind as a computer. You're hitting the delete button each time you accidentally touch that negativity key.

If you keep focusing on news indicating a bad economy, you will live in fear of loss. Bam! You'll actually bring the very thing you fear into your life.

Don't take on negative media reports or other people's fears as you allow them to become your own. Many people do this without even realizing that they just opened the door to fear and put out the welcome mat for it to enter their lives.

Even in a questionable economy, I would tell you to create a different story for yourself. Just say, "I am abundant. My prosperity is growing. All my needs and wants are taken care of at all times."

Try not to listen to any negativity. Fear and lack is negativity. Shut off negative radio and TV programs, and close those books and magazines that thrust you right into that fear state. I don't listen to the news because it's just too depressing these days. It stands to reason that if you listen to negativity, you will take some of it on and experience it in your life.

SAY YOUR AFFIRMATIONS

I'm a big believer in affirmations because they declare your life! Affirmations are a wonderful way to help you get what you want, and you should say them quite often.

Some people might ask, "What is an affirmation?" Well, an affirmation is a positive statement that declares your intentions to the Universe.

Here are a few of my favorites:

- MY LIFE IS FULL OF ABUNDANCE.

- MY LIFE IS ABUNDANT IN PROSPERITY, LOVE, JOY, AND PEACE.

- I AM BLESSED.

- I LIVE AN ABUNDANT LIFE.

- LIFE IS KIND AND GENEROUS TO ME.

- I AM GETTING PAID LOTS OF MONEY TO DO THE JOB OF MY DREAMS.

- I AM HEALTHY AND HAPPY.

- I AM IN A LOVING RELATIONSHIP WITH MY SOUL MATE.

- MY LIFE IS FULL OF HEALTH, WEALTH, AND JOY.

The trick is to change "want" to "have." Change "try" to "I am." That is, say your affirmations in the present tense. If you want something and keep saying that you want it, you will be waiting for a long time. But if you say, "I have it now," then you're telling the Universe, "I have this." And the present is when it will come to you.

Here are some things to remember when you're manifesting:

- Believe it can come true.

- Watch your thoughts, words, and emotions.

- Get rid of old belief systems.

- Say your affirmations.

- Make sure to live in gratitude.

EMOTIONS THAT YOU
NEED TO MANIFEST

Love and fear are the most powerful manifestation tools. Think of love and fear for a moment and consider how much emotion goes into both of those feelings. They are both forms of energy, but ask yourself, "Which one am I giving more power to in my life?"

Remember: Fear equals a lack of trust. If you do not trust, you will not receive.

I love the saying "Let go and let God"!

Have you ever realized that when something has been really bothering you, any attempt to control the situation never really seems to work. But the minute you let go of the situation, then it always works itself out.

That's because you let go . . . and let God!

I'd like to say a few words about worry, which is also a negative emotion. It's a way of saying, "I don't trust." You have to let go of worry to manifest anything positive in your life. You don't want to keep learning the same trust issues over and over again—do you?

Remember that worry is an old habit that you must change. It's a wasteful form of energy that can bring a lot of havoc into your life. Guilt is another waste of emotions that you'll have to let go of in order to live an abundant life.

If you feel guilty, then you will punish yourself in some way.

To help rid your life of worry, find a big bowl or vase. In fact, find two of them. One will be a Worry Bowl, and the other will be a Manifestation Bowl.

EXERCISE: Write down your worry and place it into the Worry Bowl. Now change that worry to a positive affirmation and put it into your Manifestation Bowl. For example: "I'm worried about my kids" goes into your Worry Bowl. "My kids are protected at all times" goes into your Manifestation Bowl.

Worry Bowl: "I'm worried about my bills."

Manifestation Bowl: "My payments are always taken care of, and all of my financial wants are taken care of."

Notice how I changed the word bill to payments? That's because people know that the word bill is a negative and link with it a negative emotion.

Here's an energy trick to try when it comes to making payments: I'd like you to bless them. By making a payment, you're telling the Universe that you're living in abundance because you have something to pay and you're paying it.

Keep in mind that you can fill up your Worry Bowl to the top. When you put your worries into that bowl, you're literally letting them drift out of your mind permanently.

GRATITUDE IS A MUST

I'm sure you know people who always see the glass as half empty. They truly believe that the world is out to get them. They're always complaining and never express gratitude about anything. You could say that they're living a negative life.

Gratitude is crucial. I want you to think of an area of your life that you truly are thankful for even if you have to think hard about what you're going to pinpoint. Think of something that has grown so much in love and joy and is so wonderful that you really enjoy it. This is something to express gratitude for.

Being in true gratitude opens up your heart to love, which is the most powerful manifestation tool, and will bring even more wonderful things into your life.

SELF-WORTH

The last thing I want to discuss with you before we get started is your personal self-worth. Every human being is worthy. We are all from God, and we all deserve abundance. Don't allow anyone to tell you that you're not worthy.

You'll need to rely on your self-worth when it comes to manifesting because if you don't think you're worthy enough to get what you want, then how do you convince the Universe that you are?

Let's use Donald Trump as an example. People either love him or hate him. I think of him as a great example of manifesting prosperity and abundance. He only expects the best in life, so that's what the Universe brings him. He knows he's worthy of anything, and that's why I know he will always have whatever he wants. He has an abundance of personal power, and he is powerful because that's what he tells the Universe.

I've heard many parents of top celebrities say that ever since their son or daughter was teeny-tiny, that child kept saying, "I'm going to be famous." Or the child might have said, "I'm going to be an actress and win an Oscar."

The reason those kids' dreams came true is that they believed they could achieve them. They were saying and thinking those words. They would visualize them. A powerful form of intention was going into the energy of having what they desired, and there was no doubt in their minds that they would get it.

Remember:

- Don't get jealous.

- Have it.

- Become it.

- Be it!

You can live a life of abundance just as you can live a life of struggle. I want to help you choose abundance.

Here we go!

HOW TO USE THIS BOOK

Please choose one thing that you want to manifest that you believe you can achieve in 30 days. You have to believe you can have it in order to manifest it.

And remember the following:

- You cannot manifest for others. It only works for YOU.

- Think of the upcoming 30 days as a new story for you. You're going to create your new and wonderful chapter. This is something you've been waiting for and wanting. Now you're going to say, "I have it!"

- Each day there will be an exercise to do, affirmations to say, and a visualization. Please say the affirmations out loud as many times as you can. If you're at work or around people, you can say to yourself silently.

- Feel the power in the "I am" or "I have."

- Start off your morning saying the positive affirmations out loud while looking at yourself in the mirror. You are to say the affirmations several times a day, every day, for 30 days. I will be adding more affirmations each day to add to the ones you're already saying.

- You can add your own positive affirmations, too. Just make sure they're positive and are stated as if you already have what you want.

- When you're saying the affirmations, make sure to put emotion into them. Affirmations declare your life.

- Imagine what you're manifesting as if it is already yours. Remember, the more energy you put into it, the faster the Universe will deliver it to you.

THESE ARE ALSO A MUST FOR THE ENTIRE 30 DAYS:

- Absolutely no negativity is allowed.

- Stay away from others who are negative.

- Turn off the TV and radio if they become negative.

- Remember that the news is negative, and this includes newspapers and the Internet.

- Tell all your friends and family members that you're not allowed to discuss anything negative, and you don't want to hear anything negative.

- If there is a place you dread, then stay away from it.

- Remember to say "Cancel" and then replace any negative words with positive words. For example, instead of saying, "I feel fat today" say, "My body is beautiful."

- Remember this energy trick: Put a rubber band on your wrist and snap it when you think or say a negative word. You won't want to say anything negative anymore because this hurts! Just make sure to follow it up with a positive affirmation.

- Daydream as much as you can, and while you're doing so, remember that you already have what you're manifesting.

- Pay close attention to your thoughts and words.

- Replace the words want, need, and will with have. Or simply say, "I am."

- Example: Instead of saying, "I want a new pair of shoes," say, "I have a new pair of shoes." Instead of saying, "I'm going to try to lose weight," say, "I am at a healthy weight."

- Put yourself first. Yes, first! That wasn't a typo! This doesn't mean you ignore your children or spouse. This means you need to give yourself time before you give it to everyone else. Book "you time" each day. This time might involve taking a bath or reading a book or walking the dog for 15 minutes. You have to tell the Universe that you're worthy of coming first so it believes that this is so.

- Let go of worry.

- Be open to new thought processes.

- Let go of how good things will come to you.

- Release all stress.

- Focus only on the positive and all forms of abundance.

- Say no when necessary.

- Be in control of your mind.

- If your mind starts to ramble on, meditate by yourself or with a guided-meditation CD.

- Have fun on a daily basis.

NOTE FROM VICKIE: You can do this! Trust me! After you go through this process for 30 days, you will not want to go back to the old stressed-out, worried you. Not only will manifesting bring awesome things into your life, but doing so will become easier as time progresses. You will heal areas of your life that need to be healed.

Manifesting is like going on a diet and then realizing that eating right is a way of life. The same goes for manifesting. It is a way of life.

HAPPY MANIFESTING☺

DAY 1: FIGURE OUT WHAT YOU WANT TO MANIFEST

Congratulations! You've taken the first step, and you're ready to start manifesting your dreams.

Now it's time to make it happen! Yes, this will require a bit of work because manifesting requires action.

Let's go!

The first step is easy. All I want you to do is to figure out what you want to manifest. Start with what you believe you can manifest in 30 days.

Ask yourself: What do I want? Start with something you believe is achievable in this time period. You also have to believe you can have it. Remember that it has to be for you. You cannot manifest for others.

Ask yourself: What is my dream of dreams?

_____

_____

_____

_____

_____

The key here is to be specific. It's one thing to say, "I want to be happy." It's quite another to say, "I want to open a successful business," or "I want to find the love of my life," or "I want to make a lot of money quite easily and live in prosperity this year." Your dream must be as specific as possible because the Universe likes you to recognize the details and accept them as your reality. In this case, seeing truly is believing!

MANIFEST IT: Start by asking yourself: What is the specific goal I want to manifest during the next 30 days?

_____

_____

_____

_____

_____

DO IT: Use a journal or write in this book for the next 30 days. On the first page, write down what you specifically want to manifest.

Now, let's examine your goal a bit deeper. For example, let's say your goal is that great wealth comes to you. I want you to stop and consider what money means to you. Or love? Or opening a business? Or moving to another city?

_____

_____

_____

_____

_____

What are the first thoughts that come to your mind when you think about your goal? Whatever you think of first is what I want you to jot down.

_____

_____

_____

_____

_____

Most people will have some fears that surface at this point, or age-old worries that will come to the forefront.

Let's say you were taught that people who have a lot of money are greedy. Or perhaps your parents told you to hold on to a dollar because "money is so hard to come by in life." Or perhaps you've heard that it's tough to find love after 40. You've probably also read those stories about local businesses that have gone belly up.

EXERCISE: Write down your fears involving your goal: the good, the bad, and the ugly.

_____

_____

_____

_____

_____

You will be working on your fears throughout this process. Let's go back to our money example. It's crucial to write down your fears so you can change your thinking. Just switch around what your previous misconceptions were about your goal.

The truth is that all people with money aren't greedy. And it's also true that people can also make money easily. In fact, it can just flow right to them without any hardship or struggle. You can find love by walking outside your front door.

Write down the opposite of your original thought.

_____

_____

_____

_____

_____

In this case, you would write: People with money are generous. Money does grow on trees. Love is easy to find. My business succeeds.

VISUALIZE IT: I want you to visualize people with money giving to charity. See a tree full of money. In your mind's eye, see yourself interacting with those people and plucking the money off the tree. It's fun to be original with this exercise. You can even be a bit silly and kooky here.

Now, let's say that what you want to manifest is true love during these 30 days. Instead of thinking, I'll never meet him/her, imagine your Prince or Princess Charming walking up to your door and watching a movie with you on your couch. See this person driving you to your favorite restaurant.

Now conjure up a make-believe story. Daydream, and get your emotions involved at the deepest level. Go as deep as you want because you're putting out a signal to the Universe that your dream is real and being realized by you.

- Write down what you want to manifest.

- Write down your most basic fears about it.

- Turn your words around so that you're making positive statements about your dream.

- Daydream that your wish is coming true. Get your emotions involved and go as deep as you can.

TODAY'S AFFIRMATIONS

"My life is full of abundance, and _____ is mine."

"I am fearless."

"Manifesting _____ is easy."

One Last Thing: Gently tap the top of your head and think of all the fears, ugly words, and bad thoughts you've been using to describe yourself and your life to others. Now tap out the stress. These are old belief systems that involve stagnant energy, illness, and angst. Keep tapping until you feel all of the above leaving your entire being. Take a deep breath when you're done; and see your mind, body, and life as a clean slate!

DAY 2: YOU ARE WORTHY

Even if you're not exactly sure that you're worthy of what you want to manifest, it's time to believe in yourself. I need you to work on your worthiness by pretending that you're worthy of what you want to create for yourself.

DO IT: Pretend that you're the strongest and most capable person on the planet. You're someone who gets what she/he wants in life.

EXERCISE: All day long, I want you to say, "I am worthy of _____." Then fill in the blank depending on what you want to manifest. The key here is that what you say must begin with the words I AM.

I AM are two small words that release very powerful messages to the Universe.

Some examples include:

"I am worthy of that promotion to vice president of my company."

"I am worthy of having my start-up Internet business earn $200,000 this quarter OR MORE."

"I am worthy of being in a romantic, loving relationship where all my needs are fulfilled."

"I am worthy of unconditional love."

"I am worthy of prosperity."

Today is the day that you're going to feel worthy—no matter what. Pretend that you are worthy of whatever goal you want to manifest. Affirm this by creating I AM sentences about your worth.

_____

_____

_____

_____

_____

VISUALIZE IT: Take at least 15 minutes to be by yourself. You will picture yourself in your mind as having what you want. While you're visualizing, feel the amazing emotions that coincide with your manifestation. Be as specific as you can in your imagination. Some people may not see it. They may just feel it, which is fine. It's truly the emotions that count. Make sure you imagine yourself in the picture.

TODAY'S AFFIRMATIONS

"I am worthy of _____."

"My life is full of abundance, and _____ is mine."

DAY 3: FAKE HAPPINESS

Today is your day to be happy—no matter what. It's not a time to take the Chicken Little approach where the sky is falling. On this day, you will embrace what's good in your life and be a happy person. I want you to smile, and try to keep that smile going all day long. Practice by smiling at strangers, family members, friends, and whomever you come in contact with today.

Caution: If less-than-desirable things happen today, it's your job to let them go. It's "in one ear and out the other" when it comes to forces that work against your happiness. This is the time to declare to the Universe, "I am happy today above all else."

If you're someone who naturally tends to get negative, then force yourself to focus on happiness. Your awareness of your negativity is huge today. You must be cognizant of when you're slipping off your happiness iceberg, and get right back on.

DO IT: Watch your thoughts and words carefully so you don't slip into any negativity. Rearrange your words, and change them to focus on happiness. You can even wear a little rubber band on your wrist and snap it each time you veer toward unhappiness. (I hope you're not saying "Ouch" too much!) When that negative thought comes to mind, it's your way of giving yourself a little "ping" to get rid of it. Then replace it with a positive thought.

Example: "I won't have enough money to pay the mortgage this month, and my house will surely go into foreclosure."

Revamp: "Money comes to me easily this month and covers the mortgage and all of my payments with lots of money to spare."

If you do allow a negative thought to enter your mind, then just say the words: Delete or Cancel. Change it to a happy, positive thought and word.

For example, "I will never be able to have a child" is replaced with "I get pregnant easily and have a healthy, happy baby."

Write out all the things in life that make you happy

_____

_____

_____

_____

_____

GETTING PAST A BLOCK: Watch out for other people who might try to block your manifestation. For example, let's say you're trying to be happy, but your husband takes today of all days to pick a big fight with you about balancing the checkbook or why the kitchen is always a mess or how you're always late. Consider this to be a growing time. You will still focus on happiness, but will let go of any arguments or issues until the next day. So what if he's stewing and brewing? You have to focus on yourself and change your perspective. Say, "Today is my happy day, and nobody can ruin it."

VISUALIZATION: Close your eyes and visualize going to each body part and smiling at that specific area of your body. Say to yourself, "I'm happy with my arm/leg/tummy." Visualize that body part smiling back at you. Go through every body part and organ. You will see yourself smiling at your life and your body, including the things and parts you supposedly weren't so happy with before you did this exercise. Smile! You will feel amazing. You can even sing—loudly, if you so desire! If you're happy and you know it, clap your hands. Draw smiley faces today. ☺

TODAY'S AFFIRMATIONS

"I am happy."

"My life is full of joy."

"My life is full of abundance, and _____ is mine."

DAY 4: TREAT YOURSELF

MANIFEST IT: Today you will focus on treating yourself right as a way to manifest what you want. For example, let's say you want a romantic relationship. You might want to get a pedicure, buy some sexy lingerie, or do something special for yourself because that's a way of telling the Universe that you're worthy of what you want. You're also telling yourself that you're worthy of good things.

Remember that only you can make yourself feel worthy.

DO IT: You have to take action on this day of treating yourself right. Remember that the action must be taken by you and you alone. You're saying to the Universe, "Yes, I deserve this." This might be especially hard for people who aren't used to doing anything for themselves, such as mothers who always put their children first, or those who don't have the best self-esteem.

I have clients who won't even schedule a half-hour for themselves. Of course, they're telling the Universe they're not worthy. If you don't treat yourself as if you're worthy, then the Universe won't treat you that way either.

EXERCISE: Let's say you want to manifest more money. You have to get past the mind-set that you shouldn't spend any money. There are people who have a difficult time spending any money on themselves, but you must do it. Don't necessarily buy a new car, but you can certainly go new car shopping. Then buy yourself a little treat afterward.

GETTING PAST A BLOCK: You don't have to buy yourself an expensive gift or treat yourself to something expensive. Remember that you're doing something extra special for yourself today, no matter what happens during the next 24 hours. Get a manicure and a pedicure instead of just one or the other. If you go out for lunch, then patronize a restaurant that's a little more expensive instead of the usual fast food. Do something you've always wanted to do with your free time—like going sailing. Pretend it's a date—with yourself. You aren't allowed to have any guilt when it comes to pampering yourself. If you do, then you're telling the Universe, "I don't deserve what I really want."

Today, I am going to treat myself to _____

_____

_____

_____

_____

VISUALIZATION: I want you to daydream. You will dream of the most amazing life that's full of luxury. You are a billionaire. You can do anything and go anywhere on a whim with whomever you want. You can be whatever your heart desires. Your body is amazing, beautiful, and healthy. Everyone loves you. Feel the emotions of being in awe! Get as carried away as you can. You are being pampered!

TODAY'S AFFIRMATIONS

"My life is full of prosperity."

"All my needs and wants are always taken care of."

"My life is full of magic and miracles."

"My life is full of abundance, and _____ is mine."

DAY 5: SET AN INTENTION

MANIFEST IT: You must set your intention—and then go the extra mile. Light a candle and state what you want. Write it down on a piece of paper and circle it, because a circle creates infinity. It's the circle of life.

DO IT: Watch what you write down. Make sure that you're writing what you want in the present tense, as if you already have it. Make sure to say "I am" or "I have." It's a great idea to write this down on a piece of paper or in your journal: "I AM living in abundance and prosperity. I HAVE an abundance of prosperity. I AM debt free. I AM a money magnet. I AM at the perfect weight for me. I AM beautiful."

It's good to write things down because you want to know exactly what you're manifesting. Write something such as, "I AM full of abundance, and I AM with the love of my life." Or write down, "I AM working in a new dream job making more money." Other options: "I HAVE my beautiful new bedroom set," or "I AM living in prosperity doing what I love to do."

EXERCISE: Light a candle when you're done writing what you want to manifest. Put the piece of paper you previously used under the candle and keep it there. As you light the candle, see the intention going from your heart to the Universe, and say the positive affirmation out loud. Then say, "So it is." Remember that you're writing down your intention as if you already have it.

ANOTHER INFINITY ENERGY TRICK: Write a number 8 sideways on a piece of paper and put it in your wallet or anywhere you keep money. (The number 8 written sideways is the infinity number, which means never ending.)

This will attract more money to you. You can put one in your bedroom to attract love and one in the health area of your home to attract good health. P.S.: Your health area is the center part of your home.

VISUALIZATION: Doodle number 8 sideways today and insert your intention into your doodling. Feel what you want to manifest coming to you while you're doing so.

TODAY'S AFFIRMATIONS

"There is an infinite supply of love, joy, and prosperity in my life."

"My life is full of abundance, and _____ is mine."

DAY 6: HAVE A RELEASING-FEAR DAY

MANIFEST IT: You must face your fears and have a fear day to let all of this anxiety out of your system. Ask yourself: What are my fears? You need to have your fears surface in order to move past them. There's a reason why you haven't brought what you want into your life so far, and it's probably due to your fears. Ask yourself: What am I most afraid of when it comes to getting what I want to manifest?

_____

_____

_____

_____

_____

Why don't I already have this in my life?_____

_____

_____

_____

_____

What belief system do I need to let go of that's holding me back?

_____

_____

_____

DO IT: Many of our fears are based on childhood teachings. Think about what you want to manifest, and ask yourself what you were taught about this issue as a child. Ask yourself to remember your mother's and father's fears on this topic. Most of the time your parents' fears will seep into your own belief system.

You must allow your fears to come out so you can rewrite them. For this exercise, write a contract for yourself and change the bottom line. For example, perhaps you would like to manifest a lot of money, but your mother taught you that money is evil. Rewrite a new contract, and state that money is awesome and it does grow on trees. You're basically cancelling the old thought patterns and rewriting new stories. This is a great way to release fear and push it away, so you can see a different scenario.

———————————————————

———————————————————

———————————————————

EXERCISE: You must identify your fears because they're holding you back. You want to transform the fear into trust. Ask yourself to write down the fears associated with getting what you want—and then in a separate column write a positive response. For example, maybe you're afraid that if you get a lot of money, then you will become a spoiled and selfish person. Cancel that thought by writing down that when you have money, you will enjoy your abundance and still be a kind person. Let go of the fear and transform it.

If you have a fear of abandonment, write down: "I am afraid that I will be rejected." The next sentence will be: "I am lovable." Follow it by writing: "I feel safe," and "I am safe."

Remember to write that positive statement, which will reflect your new mind-set and a place to go when you feel fear surfacing. You can also imagine a bubble with all your fears inside of it. Let the bubble get bigger and bigger until you just shove it away into outer space.

VISUALIZATION TO OVERCOME FEAR: Visualize yourself being strong, and the thing that you fear becoming an ugly monster. See yourself in your visualization. You are becoming bigger and bigger. Your body is super strong. You are much bigger and stronger than this monster you fear. The monster now has a face. It could be a stranger or someone you know. You yell at the monster, "I am more powerful than you are, and I do not fear you anymore!" See the monster of fear becoming smaller and smaller until you squash it with your foot. Feel the emotion of power throughout your whole body. You killed the fear! Yay!

TODAY'S AFFIRMATIONS

"I am fearless."

"I am strong and powerful."

"My life is full of abundance, and _____ is mine."

DAY 7: MEDITATION

MANIFEST IT: Learn to meditate in order to quiet your mind. This will only take ten minutes a day, which isn't a lot of time, but it's a great way to calm your entire being and even improve your health while helping you manifest what you want.

I know that meditating might seem intimidating for some people, but it's actually so easy to do. Just read on.

DO IT: Find a place you love to go—perhaps your backyard, a park, the beach, a quiet room in your home, or even your car, if there's no other place available. The important thing is to choose a quiet spot where you will spend five to ten minutes meditating. Nature is a great place to meditate and de-stress.

Bring an IPod with a guided meditation on it, especially if you're new to meditation. A guided-meditation CD or download will help guide you through the entire meditation process. Don't forget to bring a chair or blanket. Close your eyes. Take some deep breaths, and turn off your brain for a little while.

> **NOTE FROM VICKIE:** Meditating is not thinking, but simply giving your brain a break. Remember that all day long your brain is thinking, thinking, thinking. Your brain needs down time.

VICKIE'S EASY NO-FUSS, NO-MUSS MEDITATING METHOD: I love to meditate while taking a bath. Make it extra special by drinking a glass of wine or some tea beforehand. Play some soothing music, although it's not a must. However, music can help you let go of thoughts and stress quickly.

Remember that this is your special time. Meditation is a time to shut your brain off while you soak in the tub. To do this, just climb in, take a deep breath, and then take several deeper breaths. Visualize a blue light. You can also visualize the ocean for its blue color. Now, just clear your mind and relax.

If a thought comes in, then just see a door, open it, and allow it to leave. Another technique is to relax in bed with your bedroom door shut. Make sure it's quiet in the room so no one will bother you. Close your eyes and visualize a blue light coming in. Visualize the ocean or pretend that you're on the beach. You can also imagine you're in a forest near a blue stream. Take a few deep breaths and continue to breathe deeply.

Don't fret about meditation. You will learn more as you go, and it's easy to train yourself to relax. The more you do it, the more you will want to do it for longer periods of time. If you miss a session, you'll find yourself longing to meditate.

Remember that the key is to clear your mind, and don't allow daily worries to seep in. You will notice that the more you meditate and shut off your brain, the less drama you will have in your life.

EXERCISE: With meditation, you don't have to sit in a flowing robe and say "OM." Just get in a warm, comfortable place and lie down while stilling your mind. Play some soft, relaxing music. If you can't quiet your mind, then visualize a pause button. Hit pause on the rest of your life. Or say to yourself, "Brain, this is my five minutes. I want all thoughts out of you for five to ten minutes."

Remember to start with five minutes, and don't look at the clock. You will feel your body letting go, but you're absolutely conscious. Allow your entire body, from head to toe, to relax. While taking deep breaths, command your body to relax. Start at your head and say, "Head, relax. Neck, relax. Arms, relax. Chest, relax. Stomach, relax. Hips, relax. Butt, relax. Thighs, relax. Calves, relax. Feet, relax. Fingers and toes, relax. My whole body is relaxed!"

Think about every part of your body letting go, and the stress seeping out of each spot. Trust me when I tell you that this feels absolutely wonderful.

Remember: When your brain can't quit thinking or worrying, then your mind is in control of you and your world. You want to be in control of your mind—not the other way around.

When you bring peace to your brain by meditation and being aware of your thoughts, then you will manifest much easier.

VISUALIZATION: Send healing white light into your life. Start by seeing white light coming into your crown and going through your entire body, and then coming out of the soles of your feet. It's pushing any fear, doubt, resentment, anger, loss, illness, limiting belief systems, and stress out of your body and out of your life. The white light fills every single cell in your body.

Leave no room for anything but health and love. While seeing this light come into your body, I want you to say, "I let go of the past; as well as any fear, resentment, anger, stress, and anyone or anything that's not in my highest good. I now fill my entire life and body with love."

CLEAR THE ENERGY IN YOUR HOME: Place a bowl of water in each room of your home. Put three tea-light candles in each bowl. Do not blow out the candles. Let them burn out by themselves. Do keep a careful watch, so you don't set your house on fire! When the candles burn out, put them under water and then throw them in the trash outside of your house and dump the water down the toilet. This will cleanse your house energy and bring in peaceful, clear light.

TODAY'S AFFIRMATIONS

"I am totally relaxed."

"I am at peace."

"My life is stress free."

"My life is full of abundance, and ＿＿＿＿＿ is mine."

DAY 8: VISUALIZE WHAT YOU WANT

MANIFEST: Today I want you to go into a daydream state and visualize exactly what you want for ten minutes. Go deep into your emotions and think about how it feels to get what you want. How does it feel to have money? Visualize it coming to you, and think about what you'll spend it on. The Universe is handing it over to you.

EXERCISE: Feel little tentacles coming out of your body and bringing you what you want. Whatever it is that you want, be creative about what you visualize. Let's say you want love. This is a pretend exercise where nothing is impossible. Imagine it in any way you want it. Explore the feelings attached to getting what you want. It's crucial to feel getting what you want. Feel the love around you as a result of meeting your soul mate. Feel the wonder of holding his/her hand or touching this person's face.

If you want financial abundance, feel the money pouring down. Imagine tons of cash falling upon you. See yourself in that new job and experience the feelings you have in your corner office. How does it feel to be in there? Doesn't it feel great? Do you feel excited? Peaceful? Hopeful? In your daydream, feel every part of your dream. See the money in your hands, and picture yourself in the backyard of your new house. See your photo on the back cover of your best-selling book, and imagine the pen in your hand as you sign autographs.

TODAY'S AFFIRMATIONS

"I am living my dream!"

"My dreams are my reality."

"The Universe is very generous to me."

"My life is full of abundance, and _____ is mine."

DAY 9: SAY POSITIVE AFFIRMATIONS

MANIFEST IT: You need to get into the habit of saying positive affirmations on a daily basis—just in case you've skipped this part earlier in the book. This is a reminder to say the affirmations that are listed at the end of each day. An affirmation puts a thought into motion.

EXERCISE: I want you to look in the mirror and say your positive affirmations. Remember to say them every single day. In addition, go a step further with your positive affirmations by visualizing yourself scooping them into your heart. Pull them in with both hands. Remember that these are words and thoughts that tell the Universe you already have what you want. This process is retraining your mind. Remember that the only thing ever holding you back is your mind, and not believing you already have what you want. You are reworking your brain to believe. The faster you do so, the sooner you will have what you want.

VISUALIZE IT: Remember that everything you want is already in your energy field, or aura. So remind yourself that you have the power to get everything you want and that you never have to settle. It's up to you to take possession and believe that want you want is already yours. Once you believe that, then it will become your reality.

GREAT LOVE AFFIRMATIONS

Here are a few of my favorites for those who are manifesting love:

"I am with the person of my dreams."

"I am in a loving and joyful relationship."

"I am open for a loving relationship"

"My other half and I are so in love and full of passion."

"My love life is awesome"

"I am in a loving relationship"

GREAT PROSPERITY AFFIRMATIONS

"I am living in abundance of prosperity"

"I am a money magnet"

"Money flows to me easily at all times"

"I am always abundant in prosperity"

"My prosperity grows each day"

"I am worthy for money"

GREAT JOB AFFIRMATIONS

"I love my job"

"I am passionate about my job"

"My job is fulfilling and prosperous"

"My job is rewarding and full of abundance for me"

Vickie Emanuele

GREAT HEALTH AFFIRMATIONS

"I am healthy"

" I am at a healthy weight for me"

"My body is full of health and vitality"

"My body is filled with joy and love"

"I love myself"

"My body is beautiful and blessed"

"I listen to my body and love it"

OTHER GREAT AFFIRMATIONS

"All my needs and wants in all areas of my life are always taken care of"

"I trust in the universe to provide all my needs"

"My life rocks"

"My life is abundant in love, health, wealth, joy and prosperity"

"I am lovable and deserve only the best in life"

"Magic and miracles occur in my life at all times"

"I am blessed"

"I have an awesome life"

"Life is easy"

"My life is fun and filled with laughter"

"Kindness and generosity surrounds me at all times"

"I am surrounded by supportive, loving, kind and generous people"

"I am surrounded in beauty"

"My home is filled with peace and love"

"My life is full of peace and harmony"

"I am confident"

"I am strong"

EXERCISE: Remember to be specific in your affirmations. Write down everything you want. I do leave certain things open-ended and will always say "or more." For instance, let's say that you want to manifest an extra $100 a week. You would say, "I have $100 extra this week . . . or more!"

_____

_____

_____

Or let's say you want to lose five pounds this month. You could say, "I lost more than five pounds this month!"

If what you want to manifest is a bit more open-ended, then just say, "I want to move somewhere, but I don't know where." Or you might say, "I know I want beauty, great weather, and an ocean-side community." It's great if you make a list, stating everything that you want your new residence to be. Then you could be open-ended by saying, "In my highest good."

For example, you might say, "I'm living in the perfect city that is in my highest good." That way the Universe will give you the very best. You may not know what's in your highest good, but the Universe does.

Do not settle! Go for everything. You can manifest a wealthy, giving, and generous, loving partner just as easy as a poor, stingy, cold-hearted person.

When it comes to love, write down: "I AM with someone who is loving, kind, and gentle. I AM full of love and passion with the person of my dreams. I AM in love with my partner, and he/she is in love with me. I AM in an unconditional loving relationship." Now look in the mirror and say these affirmations.

VISUALIZATION: Imagine a bubble around you. Each time you say the affirmation, you're going to see it going into your bubble. Feel it, too! See your bubble getting bigger and bigger, and fill your emotions from the affirmations.

TODAY'S AFFIRMATIONS

"I am living in peace, love, and harmony."

"I am living in abundance and prosperity."

"I expect the best in every situation, and I get it."

DAY 10: CREATE A STORY

MANIFEST IT: It's time to write down a story on paper.

EXERCISE: You will do this in the past tense. For example, you might write: "I received a million dollars. It came to me so easily." You will create your story in this way by detailing how you manifested what you wanted easily.

You should write down your story and perhaps give it to someone you trust in a sealed envelope. Tell this person that this is an exercise to help you practice manifesting.

Again, remember to write your story as if it happened yesterday. For example: "I got a million-dollar check and went shopping," or "I sold my book, made $5 million, and have a deal for my second book. It came to me easily." The important thing is to tell the Universe that you've already achieved what you want.

Be as descriptive with your emotions as you can when you're writing these things down. Write down how awesome it was to have your dream come true easily. Allow your daydreaming to kick in. Go as far as you can with your new story. Nothing is too big! Make sure you feel the emotions of excitement, joy, and adventure. Feel the love while you're writing your wonderful new story. Don't forget to sign your name to it.

VISUALIZATION: Imagine yourself on a theater stage playing out your story. Feel all the emotions of how awesome your life story truly is. Feel how great it is to have what you want. Be as creative as you can, and be specific. How big is the stage? What are you wearing? Who's there with you? How did you get to the theater? What do you look like and feel like? See the audience applauding you. You are so happy, and they're so appreciative. Make sure to dwell on the details. And remember that you can and will have it all. No limits!

TODAY'S AFFIRMATIONS

"The story of my life is awesome."

"My life is full of abundance, and _____ is mine."

DAY 11: RENT A FUNNY MOVIE

MANIFEST IT: You want the Universe to know that you see the world as a happy, positive place that's full of joy and laughter.

DO IT: Rent a funny movie. If you love Adam Sandler, then go for it. The same goes if you want to watch Betty White in a slew of Golden Girls reruns. The point is, you must laugh. You want to watch something that's both silly and hilarious because laughter is one of the best healing tools. When you're laughing, you're not thinking of anything negative. You're in a positive mood, and your vibration is as high as it can go.

VISUALIZE IT: When you're laughing, you're tuning up your vibration to a higher level. At the same time, you're attracting higher good from the Universe. Visualize your life filled with laughter, and thus, everything will be better. You're telling the Universe that you live in a place where your smile is used often, and it feels good!

REMINDER: Be sure to say this affirmation every single day: "I am living in abundance and prosperity."

TODAY'S AFFIRMATIONS

"I am filled with laughter and joy."

"Life is easy, and I manifest everything I want instantly."

DAY 12: CREATE A VISION BOARD

MANIFEST IT: Create a vision board so that the Universe thinks you're worthy of what you desire. This is a way of training your brain to believe that your desires are already yours. That's the key to manifesting. You must believe that what you want is already in your life.

A vision board reflects your dreams of owning or being. It looks like a big collage of pictures and words. To make one, you'll need a board, which can be a box lid, sturdy construction paper, a mat, or anything you can write on or tape or glue pictures on. You can make it fancy with ribbon and jewels, or make it plain Jane. Whatever brings a smile to your face when you're done with it is exactly the right vision board for you.

DO IT: Cut out pictures from magazines, newspapers, or catalogs of what you want to manifest. Be as creative as possible. Put some time into this activity, and make a mental note to always select pictures that support your vision of the life you want to lead. Have fun with this activity, and know that there are no limits!

Let's say that you dream of bearing a beautiful child. You might want to cut out pictures from magazines of lovely, healthy, happy children playing. Or, find a picture of a pregnant woman, and paste your smiling face on top of this image. This also works with weight loss, beauty regimens, vacations—virtually anything you want to manifest.

Or perhaps you're visualizing yourself as a wealthy person. Cut out pictures that symbolize wealth, including that dream house with ten acres of land that some movie star is selling, or that foreign sports car, or that vacation spot in Paris, or a tropical beach. If you want to be a best-selling author, then cut out pictures of books that are hits and paste them on your vision board. By doing so, you're taking action and expanding your vision.

You could even print up a business card with your name and the city and state where you want to live in and put it on your board. If you want to secure a new job, print out your name, new job title, and the company you want to work for on it.

You can also write down your favorite positive affirmations and post them on your vision board. For example, you might write, "I am wealthy. Everything I desire is mine."

VISUALIZE IT: Look at your vision board often to help you visualize your dreams. Don't put it out in the garage because you're embarrassed that someone will see it. Put it up on your office wall or in your kitchen. You don't want to hide your dreams in a closet. You want the world to know that you have desires and that you're putting them on this board as a way to make them come true.

TODAY'S AFFIRMATIONS

"I am creatively manifesting my dreams now."

"I am proud of my dreams and myself."

"I accept abundance in my life graciously."

DAY 13: GO ON A NEGATIVITY DETOX DIET

MANIFEST IT: You're going to rid your entire life of negativity today. That means you will not "go to the negative," but instead, switch things around and lean toward the positive.

DO IT: During a negativity detox, you must shut out the negative forces in your life. That means getting rid of newspapers, not surfing the Web, and turning off the TV news, which is always one negative or frightening story after another. You're not going to do this every single day for the rest of your life, because that's not practical, but you are going to take a break from all the misery out there for 30 days. Trust me when I tell you that this will be one of the best moves you will ever make in your life. In addition, if you have any friends or family members who are negative people, then you're going to avoid them for 30 days.

NOTE FROM VICKIE: Do not allow negative thinking to be a part of your day. For example, banish negative thoughts such as: "I'm not good enough" or "I'm fat in these pants." If a negative thought or word comes into your mind, just say, "Cancel." Immediately transform that thought into a positive affirmation.

DISCUSS IT: During this time, you can also do an internal detox. Run it by your doctor first and ask him/her about internal cleanses or a colon cleanse. An easy cleanse is drinking a little hot water with lemon for breakfast. Another wonderful (and delicious) cleanse is taking a frozen banana and mixing it in a blender with one cup of almond milk. Add three teaspoons of flax seeds, a teaspoon of vanilla, and one packet of sugar. Add a handful of ice and blend.

You can also take a bath with Epsom salts. Add half a cup of the salts to your bath to clear away negativity. Epsom salts clear the energy field. You might wish to apply lemon-essence oil to your wrists to release negative emotions. In addition, the smell of the lemons will make you happy. It also helps clear you if you're holding onto anger.

ROADBLOCK: When those "lean toward the negative people" try to push their way back into your life—even in an innocent way—say to them in your sweetest voice, "I'm sorry, but I'm only listening to positive words. If you're negative, then I can't talk to you." If those individuals persist—for example, one of your parents, you can say, "Mom, I'm on what I'm calling a negativity detox. I have to put some boundaries up. I know you'll understand because you want me to be healthy and happy."

You can also avoid some of those negative people by saying, "I'm working on a big project right now and can't get together." In more extreme situations, you can say, "I'm only dealing with positivity right now, so I can't talk."

It's crucial to omit negativity from your life. Remember to turn off the TV the minute you hear about that "crime surge" in your area. If you can't turn it off because other family members are watching, then simply leave the room and go play with your dogs or read a positive book. When it comes to negativity, you don't want to hear it, see it, or feel it.

TODAY'S AFFIRMATIONS

"My life is full of positive expectations."

"My life is fun. I am a positive person."

"Positive situations and positive people surround me."

"I am living a positive life."

DAY 14: CLEAR THE ENERGY OF YOUR HOME

MANIFEST IT: Perhaps it's the energy in your home that's holding you back from manifesting your dreams. That's why you'll clear the energy from your living space today.

DO IT: Start by doing a major de-cluttering. If this seems too overwhelming, then begin with one area. This task is difficult for a lot of people, so you can take it one room at a time. Your goal is to make the clutter go away. Find a Feng Shui map (a bagua) and start de-cluttering the areas of your home, such as Health, Romance, and Prosperity, which align with those things you want to manifest. For example, if you want more money, you would start to de-clutter the Wealth area of your home.

Your Health area is in the center of your home, and usually in the kitchen, which makes it a crucial area to clean up. By de-cluttering, you will take all the messy energy away and allow new energy to flow. This will make a major difference when it comes to manifesting what you want. If you want new and wonderful things to come into your life, then you need to make room for them.

What will you do with what you de-clutter? Sell it, donate it, give it away, or throw it away. Good riddance!

De-cluttering can be as easy as taking one drawer out and cleaning out all the junk, which you will throw away instead of just moving it to another area.

TODAY'S AFFIRMATIONS

"Wonderful new things are coming into my life."

"I accept my newfound abundance easily."

"I have plenty of room in my life for the manifestation of my dreams."

DAY 15: LIVE IN GRATITUDE

MANIFEST IT: Being grateful is crucial when it comes to manifesting. You must be thankful for everything in your life. And you must verbally express that you're grateful for the life you're living in an honest and genuine way.

DO IT: Practice saying "Thank you" to the Universe. Also be mindful of doing kind things today, including smiling out of gratitude. If doing so isn't the norm for you, just give it a try, and I promise it will open your heart. If your heart is closed, then you're not living in gratitude. Say hello to that woman at the dry cleaners, or give a gentle smile to the man checking you out at the local convenience store. Pay the toll for the person behind you to show that you're grateful that you have the resources to do so.

Giving back to others in this lovely way will pay you back in droves. It's not only a nice thing to do, but it will make you feel so good.

> **NOTE FROM VICKIE:** Many people skip the gratitude part of their journey. You do need to be in gratitude to appreciate everything you have in life. Your blessings are everywhere, and when you acknowledge them, then more of them will come to you. Thank God.

This goes so much deeper than just saying "Thank you." It has to come from your heart. You have to be sincere in your gratitude. The problem is that when we become accustomed to good things, we always want more without thanking the Universe for what we have in the moment.

So look back on your life and express gratitude for all of the people and things and situations, both small and large. Be grateful for your partner, your children, your pets, your possessions, and the wonderful life that you might be taking for granted.

List everything you are grateful for.

_____

_____

_____

_____

_____

_____

_____

_____

_____

_____

TODAY'S AFFIRMATIONS

"I live in gratitude."

"I am grateful for my wonderful life."

"I am grateful for _____ ,
_____, and _____."

DAY 16: SPREAD LOVE TO THE AREA YOU WANT TO MANIFEST

MANIFEST IT: You need to spread a little (or a lot) of love to the area that you want to manifest. For example, if you want more money, then even if your checking account hardly has anything in it, I want you to say, "I love my bank account. It's so full." If you're trying to lose weight because your arms have always bothered you, I want you to say out loud, "I love my beautiful arms."

DO IT: Love the area of your life that you want to manifest. Start with why you love yourself. You must love yourself first and always think of yourself in a loving manner. Change any feelings you have from hate to love.

A great thing to do at dinnertime is to go around the table and have everyone express at least two things they love about their lives. If you live alone, then before each meal, say a few things you love about your life out loud.

If there's a body part you don't like, then send love to it. Instead of saying, "I hate my thighs," replace that with, "My thighs are healthy, and beautiful. They help me walk with good posture." If you desire a relationship, then focus on how much you love yourself, because loving yourself first will help you attract the love you want.

You can have a good time with this by saying words that you might have avoided in the past. Try saying, "Oh my gosh, I'm so lovable, I'm so awesome." You need to get your belief system in order by spreading this loving joy to what you want to manifest. Take a look in the mirror and say, "I love you." Make this fun for yourself.

If you put real emotion into what you're saying and feel it in your heart, then what you want to manifest will happen much faster. Remember that people who don't love themselves are telling the Universe that they're not worthy. You have to reclaim your worthiness.

DO IT- Write down a list of everything you love. Once you open the door to the things you love, many more things will come to your mind. Try to tell everyone you see today something that you love about them. "I love your smile" is a great starter. Even if you run into someone you don't like, you can find something that you love about this person, such as: "I love your shirt."

_____

_____

_____

_____

_____

TODAY'S AFFIRMATIONS

"I love my abundant life."

"I love myself."

"My life is awesome."

DAY 17: STAGE A CELEBRATION

MANIFEST IT: I know it sounds crazy, but I want you to have a celebration in advance to rejoice in what you're manifesting. When I wanted to sell a book to a certain publisher, I celebrated before it actually happened . . . and later on, it did!

DO IT: I really do want you to party on! If you don't drink, serve apple juice, invite a few friends over, and celebrate your success. You should have a toast and make sure everyone says "Cheers." Or you can just have a special dinner or dessert. Remember, the goal is to celebrate as if you've already attained your goal.

Let's say your goal is to meet your soul mate. During your celebration, you will act as if this has already happened. Say, "I have the love of my life. He/she is awesome. We're so happy together, and everything clicks for us." Likewise, celebrate that new job before it happens.

Please have fun with this, and tell your partner/friend/ mate to celebrate with you. What you're striving for is the emotion that accompanies something that has already happened. Get as creative as you can. Stand up in front of everybody and say, "I'm so excited about my new job."

What you're doing is telling the Universe that what you want has already happened . . . and then it will become a reality for you. You're just fast-forwarding it in your head and heart. The way to get everything you want is to already be thankful. That vibration is key. Plus, your celebration will be so much fun! Cheers!

TODAY'S AFFIRMATIONS

"I am celebrating my new _____."

"I am living my dream."

"My life is fulfilling."

DAY 18: VISUALIZE BEFORE YOU GO TO BED

MANIFEST IT: You need to see it to believe it.

DO IT: Before you go to bed at night from now on, I want you to visualize how you will feel after your dream has come true. Remember, it has already happened! It's your reality. I love doing this before bedtime because this is a time when you can easily relax and enjoy what you're doing without any interruptions. You're also training your brain to imprint what you're manifesting. I recommend visualizing during the day, too, for a little extra push.

For example, if you want financial abundance, then see yourself with the cash. What are you spending the money on? How does it feel to have it? Pretend you're in a movie playing the part you've cast yourself in. Visualize as many things as you can. Experience the emotions, and note how great it feels to be playing your part. Now go to sleep with a smile on your face. These thoughts will be lurking in your subconscious all night long.

TODAY'S AFFIRMATIONS

"I have all my needs and wants . . . and more!"

"I am experiencing my desires."

"I am living my dream life."

DAY 19: REPLACE YOUR WORDS

MANIFEST IT: By this point, you might need a little refresher. Remember to replace "I want" with "I have" or "I am." You're asking the Universe for what you want from a place where you already have it.

DO IT: Remember to be very specific about what you have or what you are. For example, instead of saying, "I want a new love," change your words to the very specific, "I have an amazing new love who came to me easily and effortlessly. It's so wonderful."

Or perhaps you dream of becoming an actor. Say, "I am acting in a Hollywood movie, and it came easily and effortlessly to me." Use your daydreams to convince you that you're living the life you want.

If you want to be an author, see your book cover and talk about it in the past tense:. "I'm a best-selling author, and my book signing went so well." When you start to really believe that your dream has already come true, then it will happen.

Write out your NEW words to confirm your manifestation.

_____

_____

_____

_____

_____

On an emotional level, I want you to feel that you already have what you want. Take your hands and place them in front of you. Visualize that what you want is in your hands, and imagine that your hands are magnets pulling what you want toward you. Put your heart into this exercise, and truly experience these awesome emotions. Feel a smile coming over your face as you give yourself what you want.

TODAY'S AFFIRMATIONS

"My life is full of gifts."

"I love giving to myself."

"I love my abundant life."

"I have all that I want and need at all times."

DAY 20: TAKE ACTION

MANIFEST IT: It's one thing to ask the Universe for what you want. But you must always take action.

DO IT: Let's say that you want a new car—a large, amazing SUV. You need to take action by going to a car dealer to shop for that new vehicle. Or let's say that you want to be wealthy. You might go to a very expensive boutique and make a list of what you will spend your money on.

I want you to say, "I can afford this." When you're resonating that vibration, what you want will actually be brought to you. Feel the amazing joy of buying that SUV or that Chanel bag. Feel the joy of a new romance.

But you do have to leave the house and take action. Play the part of someone who can afford anything if that's what you're manifesting. If you want a new romance, actually go to a club or engage in a certain activity you like, acting as if this is where you've met your soul mate.

This is also a good time to ask for guidance from a higher power. Ask Spirit and your angels for help. Ask what you need to do to make your dream come true. This might involve sending résumés or getting referrals from others who are in the field. You might play the Lotto or look into a second job. If you want love, think outside the box and engage in an activity that you love. I met my husband playing softball. I would never have met him if I'd stayed at home lying on the couch. That's why you need to take action. Then let go . . . and let God.

My action is going to be?

_____

_____

_____

TODAY'S AFFIRMATIONS

"I am taking action toward realizing my dreams."

"I manifest my dreams easily and effortlessly."

"I am an abundance magnet."

DAY 21: PAMPER YOURSELF

MANIFEST IT: In order to tell the Universe that you're worthy of what you want, you have to treat yourself as if you are worthy.

DO IT: This is a day to engage in some self-love and pampering. This is hard for a lot of people, especially mothers. They don't want to pamper themselves because they would rather spend money on, or pay attention to, their kids. Wrong! If you're in bad health or not taking a little time to pamper yourself, then who will take care of your kids if you get sick? When you're constantly putting yourself last, you're telling the Universe that you're not worthy.

So pamper yourself!. A spa weekend is a great way to make this happen, or even just a day walking through a beautiful park or strolling on the beach if you can't afford to go away. Whatever you do that soothes your soul is a way of pampering yourself. When you indulge in self-love, then the Universe will return the favor tenfold.

Other suggestions: get an hour-long massage, have your nails done, allow your mate to give you a back rub, or read a favorite book. The idea is to announce to yourself and the Universe that you're worthy of everything you want.

Remember, if you tell the Universe that it's okay to put yourself last because you do that every day, then the Universe will listen to you. If you're giving away all of your energy, you will also grow resentful and angry. Give to yourself first and then you'll have so much more to give to everyone else. Think of this as pampering your soul.

I am going to pamper myself today by

_____

_____

_____

_____

_____

TODAY'S AFFIRMATIONS

"It is easy to pamper myself and give to myself."

"I love myself."

"I am worthy of all of my desires."

DAY 22: CLEAR YOUR ENERGY FIELD

MANIFEST IT: You'll need to continually work on clearing your energy field. Your task will be to remove any old, negative, or cluttered energy from your home, your office, and your being. When I talk about dead energy, it's that feeling you get when you walk into a room and feel completely stymied. You feel blocked and the air seems dead. That's bad energy, and it's time to become your own one-person clean-up crew. (Note: These are great exercises to do on a continual basis.)

DO IT: You can clear energy in several simple ways that will have amazingly transformative effects. One of my favorites is to add Epsom salts to a bath to clear your personal energy. When it comes to clearing the energy of a room, use sage and smudge pots because they do wonders. These items can be found at metaphysical establishments and in certain health stores.

Smudging is an old Indian tradition that clears energy. You smudge by lighting sage and blowing it out until it smokes. Once it does so, go around your entire home with the windows open. Concentrate on the rooms that don't feel peaceful and that have a lot of electronic devices that disrupt the peace. Leave the windows open for a couple of hours afterward to let out the negative or stale energy. What will remain is peaceful, white-light energy.

After smudging, you can also bring in clear, happy, white light by burning three tea lights in a bowl of water made of glass. When they burn out, place the cool tea lights in the trash outside and dump the water down the toilet. You can do this in each room and in your office. I promise you that the energy will feel amazing after you do this exercise.

I do this in my house at least once every month. The energy that remains is absolutely awesome. This will not only clear energy, but it will help with stress and sleeping. One note: make sure you're home until all the candles burn out.

What you're doing with the smudge pots and tea lights is clearing out the negative energy, which allows positive energy to come in. Another simple clearing technique is to put out a small bowl of water filled with a cup of sea salts. Or, put pretty flowers in your home office to clear out negative work experiences. If you feel that there is dead energy in a certain portion of a room, such as a corner, then make sure to put some real (not fake) plants in that area. A water fountain will also lift the energy and create better energy.

Music works well, too. If your room has dead energy, then play some upbeat music in that room even if you're not there at the time.

Whatever path you take to clear the energy, you must do it. Just like a computer gets fragmented, so does the energy in various places. Don't allow the energy surrounding you to become clouded or stale.

TRY IT: People also have an energy field, which is why I mentioned bathing with Epsom salts, which is a natural way to clear energy. Remember that all negative thoughts just add to the clutter in your energy field, so you must get rid of them.

Just imagine yourself taking a big broom and literally sweeping the negativity away. Think to yourself that you can see a white light coming through the crown of your head and following a path where it goes to all areas of your body. Imagine the white light as it flows from your head, down your neck, into your chest, and beyond, until you reach your toes. As the white light works its magic, imagine how it's clearing your energy field and pushing all the stale, yucky stuff out through the bottom of your feet. This is a great way to mentally shove out all the stress that has been bothering you, too, which also mucks up your energy.

TODAY'S AFFIRMATIONS

"My energy is clear and happy."

"Life is full of beauty."

"My life has an abundance of flowing, positive energy."

"I am living a joyous life."

DAY 23: PLAY MUSIC

MANIFEST IT: It's important when manifesting to train your mind to shut off. That way what you're trying to manifest will be at the forefront.

DO IT: An easy way to shut off your mind is to play some kind of healing music (classical or New Age, perhaps). Music is an easy way to get you out of your head. It lifts your vibration and allows new energy to flow to you.

If you prefer rock music, that will also work, and please feel free to jam out or sing with the music, which is also cleansing because you can't easily worry about much else when you're singing Bruce Springsteen or Madonna songs loudly. The idea here is to turn off the worry, so feel free to turn up the volume!

Vickie Emanuele

It's a good idea to try different musical styles until you find what works for you. If you want to dance, then move to your heart's content. Music has a unique vibration that really makes your energy field feel vibrant, too. I know many people who need more of a mellow type of music to bring their energy down. If you're naturally hyper, then try to go the mellow music route and put on something soothing. The point is, you're going to release stress while actually balancing your chakras in the process. It's a win-win-win! By the way, I challenge you to be in a bad mood after listening to your favorite music!

Everyone benefits from music that clears the chakras. There are all kinds of guided chakra-clearing CDs and downloads. Get comfy on your bed or somewhere you feel relaxed, and enjoy the sounds. You will feel amazing afterward. Clearing your chakras cannot be done too often. Make it a regular part of your routine.

TODAY'S AFFIRMATIONS

"My vibration is awesome."

"My life is clear and balanced."

"I feel happy and relaxed."

DAY 24: EXPLORE YOUR CREATIVITY

MANIFEST IT: In order to manifest, you need to tap into your passions. This day is important even if you don't think of yourself as a creative person. It's about exploring a side that allows your passions to go from thoughts to actual expression.

DO IT: How can you have a morning or afternoon where you explore creativity if you don't sing, paint, dance, or write? Don't worry about being perfect here. This is about exploration. I'd like you to also realize that you're killing your soul if you deny yourself creative expression.

Everyone can sing—even a little bit. If you've always wanted to learn how to dance, then take a few lessons or go out dancing with the girls. Who cares if you're not ready for Dancing with the Stars? Just become a star in your own mind. Let your inner child come out to play, and have fun with your creative endeavors. Try a Zumba class and make up a few of your own steps. The goal here is to open up your passion chakra, which will help you manifest more than you could ever imagine.

Remember that anything creative works here. Yes, cooking a pot of chili can be a creative outlet, too! You're becoming an abundant, positive-thinking person who is creative in different ways. One of my favorite creative moments is to try pottery and get my hands dirty. Gardening is another great outlet. You're basically telling the Universe, "Hey, I'm willing to do something new!" Have fun with it!

TODAY'S AFFIRMATIONS

"My life is full of passion."

"I am creative."

"I love using my creativity."

DAY 25: GET SOME SUPPORT

MANIFEST IT: It's helpful to get a little support at this point of the manifesting journey.

DO IT: Have a manifesting night at your house—a party where maybe just two or three friends come together to support each other's dreams. You should agree to celebrate your achievements as if they've already happened. For example, tell your friend Mary, who hopes to write a best-selling novel, "I saw your book at Barnes & Noble today. It was almost sold out."

Yes, you can do this yourself, but it's great to get some support. One tip: choose support partners who have similar vibrations and outlooks on life. You can also help each other in various other ways. For example, if you want to lose weight, then choose support members from your Weight Watchers group. Or, if you want to earn more money, find friends in the same boat and not your pal who's already enjoying an inheritance and doesn't need more cash. That is, gather people together who have similar wants and desires.

A NOTE FROM VICKIE: Make sure you don't choose support people who are jealous of you—you want those who want the best for you. Figure out beforehand through some simple conversations if your support people are true friends who are sending positive energy your way. These people need to be encouraging, and this must come from their hearts.

TODAY'S AFFIRMATIONS

"I am ＿＿＿＿＿＿."

"I have ＿＿＿＿＿＿."

"My dreams are being fulfilled."

"I am worthy of manifesting ＿＿＿＿＿＿."

"＿＿＿＿＿＿＿＿ is on its way to me now."

DAY 26: CUE THE VIDEOTAPE

MANIFEST IT: One great way to manifest is to videotape or film what you desire. Since most of us have smart phones that can turn us into mini Steven Spielbergs, this should be an easy, inspiring (and also transforming) technological task.

DO IT: Film yourself—even for a few minutes—living your dream. If you desire money, perhaps you film yourself drinking a glass of champagne and talking about your new vacation home. If you desire a soul mate, then video yourself describing this person and how you've just had the most romantic evening together.

Telling your story on video is quite powerful. You can play it back and watch it as a way to affirm what you're manifesting. If you find this hard to do or embarrassing, be content in knowing that only you will watch it. It doesn't have to go viral!

Personally, I videotaped myself at a "book-signing party," where I said I'd just sold five million copies of my new book, and my publisher was demanding the next one.

And then there was a client I had who'd always wanted a Rolex. He couldn't afford one, but he did buy a fake Rolex that he used in his video. One month later, he had a financial windfall that allowed him just enough cash to buy a real Rolex.

I can't stress this enough: remember to visualize what you're manifesting as if it has already happened. That's how the Universe will know what to bring you!

TODAY'S AFFIRMATIONS

"My life is full of miracles."

"All of my wants are provided at all times."

"I am totally fulfilled."

DAY 27: HAVE A MAGIC DAY

MANIFEST IT: Everyone needs magic in their lives! If you don't believe in magic, then how will you bring it into your life? Today is the day you get to play with magic.

DO IT: Create a magic wand, or even a pencil will do. Make sure you're clear that your intention is to transform that pencil into a magic wand. Think of yourself as a magician. Imagine that what you've been waiting for will just appear out of thin air. You can make a magic wand out of sticks, glue, stones, ribbon, and glitter. It doesn't matter how it looks. It's all about the intention you're putting into it.

After you're done creating the wand, create a magic altar. An altar doesn't have to be anything fancy. It can just be a card table that you throw a runner over, or you can use your nightstand. You can make your altar as fancy as you want. Remember, this is your altar only! Hands off to everyone else.

Put your vision board on your magic altar. You can also place anything else on it that represents what you want to manifest. Remember to start with just one thing to manifest.

Let's say you want to manifest money. Put some money on the table, and pictures or figurines of the things you want the money to buy. If you want a new car, then get a toy car that looks like the one you want. If you crave more peace in your life, then lay something down that represents peace to you, like a hand-drawn peace sign or a candle.

Now you're going to perform a magical ritual. Begin by writing down what you want (as if it has already happened) in a circle on a piece of paper. Include your full name.

For example, if I wanted a new job, I would write: "Vickie Emanuele has a wonderful new job that I'm so passionate about. It's a dream job for me. I am making tons of money doing what I love to do. I am working when I want to work." Remember to write something like this in the circle.

Place this on the magic altar, because that's where everything comes true! Light a candle on your magic altar if you'd like. Now take your magic wand, even if it's a pen or pencil, and wave it at the magic altar, saying aloud three times (start saying it softer and ending the third time saying it louder) what you just wrote. See and feel your intention going out into the Universe, and the magic coming back into your life with your dream manifested! When you're done, say, "And so it is."

Visit your altar often and feel the magic in it. The more you use your wand, the more power will come into it. You can leave this magic altar standing, with the intention that anything you put on it will appear in your life. Watch what you wish for . . . because it will come true.

TODAY'S AFFIRMATIONS

"My life is full of magic."

"Magic is appearing in my life in many ways."

"My life is full of miracles."

"_____has appeared in my life easily."

DAY 28: VALIDATION DAY

MANIFEST IT: Today is your validation day. Everything is good. You're aware that what you've manifested is actually coming true or already has come true. You're going to take this day to validate that what you manifested is very real.

DO IT: Proceed through this day as if what you've manifested has already happened. I remember once when I manifested kindness. Sick and tired of living in a hostile world, my goal was for people to simply act nicer. On my validation day, I lived as if the world was already a kind place. Just believing that in my mind made it true in very real ways. People opened doors for me all day, and a friend said, "Let me buy you lunch." My goal was to surround myself with kind and loving people. On this day, my clients actually brought me several gifts, although they were unaware that I was validating myself.

Your goal today is to look for signs in the Universe that validate that what you've manifested will come true. A friend of mine was engaged to a man and looking forward to moving in with him instead of spending half her life on the busy 101 California highway to get between their two homes. She wanted to manifest the perfect home for the two of them. On her validation day, she went house hunting with a Realtor and didn't even need to see the inside of a certain house at 101 Blueberry Lane. Of course, the interior was perfect, as was the entire home, which she and her fiancé quickly purchased without any hassles. The Universe sent her a clear sign that she was being validated, and that there would be no more "long distance" in that relationship. The 101 number on the house was the bridge between their two worlds.

Write down things that you have noticed coming into your life since you started on your manifesting journey.

_____

_____

_____

TRY IT: Write down in a journal each time the Universe validates what you're trying to manifest. It's great to look back and see how easy it was to make your dreams come true.

TODAY'S AFFIRMATIONS

"I am _____."

"I have _____."

"The Universe supports me in whatever I want to do."

"All my dreams come true instantaneously."

DAY 29: EXPLORE ACCEPTANCE

MANIFEST IT: So many people manifest what they want and find it hard to accept what they've done. On this day, it's time to accept your bounty of good fortune. This is easier said than done for those of us who have conditioned ourselves to accept "less than best" and "make the most of it." I want you to toss out that old thinking, because that tells the Universe that you deserve less. It's crucial to not only rejoice, but to accept that you deserve EVERYTHING and MUCH MORE!

DO IT: Acceptance is huge, because you have to be open, willing, and ready to receive whatever you want so you don't sabotage yourself. For example, a lot of people say they want a great relationship and then they actually do manifest a wonderful partner. But do they accept it? No! Instead, they nitpick and try to destroy the relationship because deep down they're afraid they're not worthy of the good that has come to them.

You need to work on just allowing the good to flow to you. If you receive, you don't always need to give the "giver" a gift. Instead, I'd like you to simply say, "Thank you." For example, you can say, "Thank you, Universe. I accept this money as my way of being grateful for abundance." This actually gets much easier as you get older.

DO IT: Sit or lie down with your palms open and facing up. Close your eyes and say out loud, "I am open and ready to accept _____ into my life now." Visualize the thing you've been manifesting coming into your hands. Now say, "Thank you for giving me _____," and hold the visualization of what you just received into your life for at least five minutes while taking ownership of it.

TODAY'S AFFIRMATIONS

"I accept and appreciate all the generosity and kindness in my life."

"I accept all that is good."

"My life is full of kind and giving people."

"I accept love easily."

"I am so happy that _____ has become my reality."

DAY 30: AN ATTITUDE OF GRATITUDE

MANIFEST IT: You already did manifest it—congratulations!

DO IT: Give yourself a big pat on the back! You've changed who you are, and are now a more positive person who knows that dreams can easily come true. Applaud the good in your life. Take a few minutes to be grateful for what you've been given. Make sure to celebrate your efforts and be proud of yourself.

I am grateful for?

_____

_____

_____

_____

_____

_____

_____

_____

_____

_____

Don't allow that feeling of gratitude to leave you. Make an effort to turn around your negativity. Don't be a grouch. Stay focused on the positive, and act grateful. Write down what you love about your life. Are you grateful for your mate? Your children? Your pets? Your work? Your home? The Universe will acknowledge your next request only if you're a grateful person who appreciates the beauty of this earth.

I regularly say things such as: "I'm grateful for my health, my eyesight, my hearing, and the way I can run down the beach with my children." I pinpoint something new each day and say it out loud. So make your own gratitude list—and change it often.

Remember, once you start to be more grateful, then more and more goodness will come to you. Let it flow!

TODAY'S AFFIRMATIONS

"I am so grateful for all that I have and all that I am."

"My new _____ is awesome"

"I am a manifesting Queen/King."

FINAL THOUGHTS FROM VICKIE

Congratulations! You've completed your 30-day manifestation journey. You know that the doors to the Universe are open, and you now know how to walk through them.

By now, manifesting should be a part of your life. You know how to do it . . . and you can do it again and again throughout all the days to come.

Manifesting should now be a habit for you. It's a way of living that you've truly mastered. So don't feel shy about asking for the next treasure in your life. The Universe is just waiting to give it to you as a way to feed your soul and turn your dreams into reality.

Each time you practice manifestation, it will become easier, and the results will happen more quickly.

DREAM BIG!

Until next time,

Vickie

P.S.: Please drop me a line at energyreader1@ yahoo.com. Please share with me and others what you manifested after reading this book. I will share amazing manifesting stories on my website www. energyreader.com, or find me on Facebook.

*** ***

ABOUT THE AUTHOR

Vickie Emanuele is an internationally recognized energy reader and healer for people and pets.

Vickie is an energy expert. She reads into the energy of past, present and future to help in all areas of life. Vickie also has the gift to communicate to loved ones in heaven, angels and spirit guides.

Vickie's energy healings on people and pets can be performed in person or remotely by tapping into their energy field. Energy healings help with health, illness, disease, stress, removal of energy blocks, past lives, negative energy cords, weight, hormone imbalance, balance issues and overall body, mind and soul wellness.

Vickie's animal readings help with health, behavior, allergies, and overall wellness. Pets benefit from energy healings as well as their owners.

Vickie holds Energy workshops, webinars, medium galleries and is available for private readings and energetic energy healings.

Her passion is to educate people to playfully tap into their intuition to improve their energy to live a joyful, healthy, abundant life. She believes everyone deserves abundance in all areas of life!

Vickie lives in California enjoying her 5 children and being outside in nature. She loves hiking, water sports, gardening, animals and all the beauty earth has to offer. Playing in the magic of energy is a passion she enjoys every day.

Contact Vickie through her website at www.energyreader.com or by email energyreader1@yahoo.com. Become a Fan on Facebook at www.facebook.com/EnergyReader for manifestation and energy tips.